Blueprint
Your Future

Blueprint Your Future

Creating Powerful Personal and Career Results Through Alignment and Action

Susan Bosscawen

Butterfly Publishing

For more information please visit:
www.blueprintyourfuture.com

Book design by:
www.arborbooks.com

Printed in the United States of America

Blueprint Your Future:
Creating Powerful Personal and Career Results through Alignment and Action
Susan Bosscawen

1. Title 2. Author 3. Self-Help/Career

Library of Congress Control Number: 2009900441

ISBN 10: 0615273912
ISBN 13: 978-0-615-27391-4

For my sister Maria.

Table of Contents

Foreword
by
Phil Krause
Phil Krause and Associates
Performance Consulting

The idea for this book came out of a conversation that Susan and I had over lunch. We were talking about career aspirations, goals and plans for the future. She told me about a process she had used many times in business planning to define business strategies and actionable plans. As we talked, we realized how the process could be adapted to help people fulfill their potential, and how much they might benefit.

Since then, I have used the process and materials with many of my clients and the feedback from those experiences shows that this topic matters to a lot of people, because down deep humans really do want to pursue their aspirations when they have the right tools to do so.

But as you look at this book, you may be wondering, "Why another self-help book?" or "How can this book help *me*?"

Well, if you're like most people, many of the changes in your life and career have resulted from "accidents"—that is, you've reacted to problems or responded to opportunities that have come your way rather than planning for them. Consequently, you're not likely to be where you really want to be—or where you *could* be.

And you're not alone. In my thirty years as a consultant, I have learned that most clients don't call or seek help until they're experiencing a certain amount of pain. It's the same in their personal lives. People get used to "going with the flow" so often that they rarely assert control by challenging themselves to get out of their rut or to set specific goals in the major areas of their lives. If that sounds like you, you're reading the right book.

Do you find yourself rationalizing your station in life—regarding your career, family, health, etc.? If so, that means you're normal. It probably even seems logical to suppress your hopes and dreams when you can't see how you could ever reach them from your current situation or when you don't know the steps it will take to achieve them. You may even be worried about the effort it will take to get where you want to be.

Sound familiar?

If nothing else, this book can restore your hope by providing you with a new logic that will help you clarify what you really want, by determining what you realistically need to get there, and by helping you appreciate, and leverage, what you already have going for you.

If you follow the process explained in this book, you can "connect the dots" and build some positive momentum by developing a plan for moving from point A to point B, then acting on it. These small wins, the ones where you make consistent improvements, add up and ultimately you arrive at point Z, a place where you can be the person you want to be.

Remember that this is not a zero-sum game: Having a "plan" doesn't mean you still can't take advantage of those "accidents." In fact, your plan will help you sort through opportunities to better know which ones to pursue.

One memorable incident about lost ambition happened during a workshop I conducted several years ago. During a break, a middle-aged participant—a very successful, well-compensated banking executive—came up to me. With a somewhat wistful look, he said, "It just dawned on me that what I really enjoy is doing deals. Unfortunately, because I was so successful at doing deals, I now manage people who manage people who manage people who do deals—so I don't get to do what brings me the most satisfaction. I feel trapped, and I don't see any way out of it."

Have you ever felt "trapped" like that? Have you ever caught yourself making comments like these?

- "This isn't what I had planned for my life."
- "How did I get here, anyway?"
- "Is this as good as it gets? There must be something better."
- "I really don't want to be doing this for the rest of my career."

Often, a sigh of resignation accompanies the above remarks. If that describes your situation, what can you do about it?

Of course, no less-than-desirable situation happens overnight, so don't expect to turn things around by simply reading this book. But there are actions you can take *today* to begin the process of becoming the person you really want to be—and this book will help you achieve that outcome.

Throughout this book, the term "alignment" is used to describe a state in which your everyday behaviors are in sync with your values and your actions are moving you toward your aspirations. Having alignment can give you the sense that what you are doing—in your life and career—is what you *want* to do, and more importantly, what you *ought* to be doing. As Joseph Campbell once wrote:

> *If you follow your bliss, you put yourself on a kind of track that has been there all the while, waiting for you, and the life that you ought to be living is the one you are living. Wherever you are—if you are following your bliss, you are enjoying that refreshment, that life within you, all the time.*

Do you wonder if alignment is worth it—or doubt that it can produce "bliss"? Consider a time in your life when you felt that what you were doing at work, at home, etc. was your "highest and best use," and that whatever you were doing justified why you were put on this Earth. To fall back on a cliché, you were "at one with the Cosmos." What was that like? How did you get there? Why didn't you remain in that state? If this describes your life now, congratulations! You can feel good about where you are—and use this book to help keep you there.

As you work through this process, you will answer a lot of questions about what you have going for you and what your aspirations and goals are. One way to test the process is to consider successful career or life transitions you've initiated in the past to see if you went through similar steps—and understand how they helped you achieve your goal.

Of course, there are many books and speakers out there that can pump you up or make you feel good (temporarily) by telling you, "You have what it takes to be successful"—but what do you do when you finish the book, or the workshop ends, or the motivational speaker walks off the stage? This book can bridge the gap from head to heart to hands by giving you the tools to clarify your thoughts and feelings and identify high-impact actions you can take to achieve your goals and aspirations.

Once you establish positive momentum in the right direction, you'll probably surprise yourself with how much you can achieve. As Henry David Thoreau said:

> *If one advances confidently in the direction of his dreams, and endeavors to live the life which he has imagined, he will meet with a success unexpected in common hours.*

Before you start, keep in mind: It's more of a journey than a destination and we want to make sure you're on the right path at the right time with the right tools, moving in the right direction.

Introduction

The premise of this book is a simple one: Start with a thorough look at "you" and then begin building your options. The objective being to look at "you" from every angle so that you can compare and contrast your aspirations and goals, competencies and opportunities, resources and assets—first generally and then specifically.

The ultimate goal of this book is to teach you how to achieve alignment in planning your personal and career goals. Being in alignment means knowing that the actions you take today, tomorrow and next week are undertaken with a purpose in mind; that they are designed to help achieve your goals and aspirations.

Having alignment means having a purpose and a drive tied to goals and an actionable plan. With the alignment you achieve through building your Blueprint Action Plan™ you will be able to know that what you do each day is for a specific reason and that it is helping you advance toward being the person you've always dreamed of being.

Throughout the process laid out in this book you will ask the "what if?" question over and over and validate your commitment to what could be your future. The "what if?" question in the context of this book is thought-provoking and liberating, not limiting. It will become encouraging and engaging, not intimidating. You won't be asking "what if?" in a way that laments what might have been. You will be asking the question in a way that examines the possibilities in your future.

The pictures you develop as you examine yourself will provoke thought and allow you to examine your choices more deeply. You can explore the effects of certain choices and change those choices based on further thinking. You will use the work you do through this book to create a picture of you and a Vision-to-Action Framework™ of choice. You will build confidence as you gain a clearer understanding of you and your choices. The future becomes less daunting and more hopeful as your path forward is lit with self-knowledge and abundant choice.

Armed with the knowledge of "you," your understanding of aspirations and goals, opportunities and interests, competencies and talents, you can be better prepared to survive and even thrive in today's economic climate. You will feel more confident and prepared for the future. You will be fully cognizant of your choices and you will understand the actions required to realize your goals and aspirations through well-thought-out opportunities and specific areas of focus.

At several points during this process you will test your yourself to ensure your commitment to your aspirations and goals. Then, you will put it all together in a Blueprint Action Plan™. This plan will help you realize that your success is at hand. Through focused intention and the right effort your goals and aspirations will become reality.

The Vision-to-Action Framework™

The process of putting together this valuable picture of you is based on a combined sixty years of experience. Over those years, we have coached hundreds of people and amassed the knowledge necessary to help people through this process in a straightforward, positive, actionable way.

The Vision-to-Action Framework™ is the basis for this picture of you. The use of the Vision-to-Action Framework™ has been a work in progress for over fifteen years. Applied in a business environment, it proved valuable as a tool to bridge strategy and tactics. We have taken this concept and modified it to apply in a personal and career-planning context.

This knowledge has been combined with an understanding of how to construct a process for examing the elements of choice and creating a repeatable process. Years of collective knowledge from business practices have been leveraged and made it relevant to personal choice. The results at each step have been kept fresh and can be refreshed at any time with deeper thought and understanding of choices.

The processes of thinking, refining and challenging have been embedded throughout the book to ensure your commitment to the goals you outline and a successful result. Additionally, case studies have been included throughout to provide you with examples and key learning on how to think about the exercises.

Making significant career and personal changes can be challenging. People are creatures of habit and sometimes change is uncomfortable. So you're probably asking, "Why now? Why should I be embarking on a journey like this in the midst of a turbulent economy, a difficult business climate and an uncertain job market?"

If you read the foreword then you probably know at least some of the reasons why right now is as good a time as any to examine your present circumstances in order to identify some of your choices and opportunities. But in today's environment of uncertainty it may be difficult to imagine that this could be the best time to take stock of where you are and what you want to do in the years ahead.

But this is precisely the moment to do that. The challenges that businesses are facing are forcing corporate leaders to make tough choices and usually that means tough decisions about investments, jobs and employees. You're probably acutely aware of this, whether you already have a job or want to get a job. You wonder where the job opportunities are or how to prepare for any number of situations leading to job change or personal change. You know that making sense of the situation would help, but how?

While this isn't the most pleasant of times, it can be one of the most productive for you personally if you know your options and can prepare to take action when opportunities arise!

"**What if?**" It's a question on everyone's mind, especially now. And it doesn't seem to matter their circumstances.

Your career may be the product of hard work, a growing economy, a growing company and great opportunities. You may never have had to contemplate "what if?" But a lot has changed. The current climate is not comfortable.

You may be seeking a job, finding the opportunities limited and contemplating what this climate may mean long-term. Or you may just want a change in your personal life and a fresh start.

The thought of "what if?" can be daunting and discouraging as it suggests tough choices. But you can make the best of the situation if you have the tools to make sense of your options. In fact, the hope is that this question can be liberating and compelling as you realize you have options *and options provide hope.*

Clearly identifying your options for the future and then evaluating those options in a straightforward, well-thought-out manner can help you prepare for the future with confidence. The decisions you make every day are driven by the choices you make of one thing over another.

Having a clear understanding of the basis for these options, as well as having alignment with your aspirations and goals and having timeframes and the commitment needed, can only enhance the probability that you will make a good choice, select the right option and have a successful outcome. Equally important is understanding the risks associated with certain options and how reducing that risk might save you from a costly and painful experience. This knowledge will give you confidence and inspire you with a more positive attitude about the future and turn hope into a strategy.

The analysis you are asked to do in this book has been combined with the construction of a unique Blueprint Action Plan™ that crystallizes your thinking into choices that are actionable. After all, what is the purpose of defining your goals if you don't build a plan to attain them?

The Blueprint Action Plan™ is a new, powerful concept. The blueprint allows you to see the power of aligning your choices with your values and priorities AND shows you how to get started on bridging the gap between where you are and where you want to be. The action plan will keep you on track with timeframes and key progress points. This no-nonsense, business-based approach to creating your personal blueprint is the result of our collective experience and learning with hundreds of clients and associates. Right now is the time to put this learning to use to help you shape your future.

A Footnote to the Journey

This is a journey and not an event, so you will need to engage with an open and willing mind and be committed to investing some time. It might take you several days to put your Blueprint Action Plan™ together, but it is time well-invested. At times this may be hard work. It should be. You are investing in yourself by examining you from a lot of different angles. The work should be thoughtful and thought-provoking. But the result will take you forward into the future with a sense of optimism and direction and better prepare you for today's challenges.

Hopefully you will find examining your choices and performing the analysis that follows productive and inspirational. At the very least, may you find surprising and exciting options as you blueprint your future!

A Short Summary of the Process

This book is designed to help you align your actions with your aspirations—bring action and alignment together. The process involves a self-assessment that helps you discover where you want to be and which actions you might take to align yourself to your goals and aspirations. Here is a brief, step-by-step summary of the process. You may not be familiar with some of the terms yet, but as you go through the book, each step will build upon the previous one.

Assess Your Current Situation:
Start by determining your current values, talents and competencies. With your critical few selected, you'll begin to build the Vision-to-Action Framework™. This self-assessment is foundational to the whole process.

The Vision-to-Action Framework™ looks like this:

Vision to Action Framework™

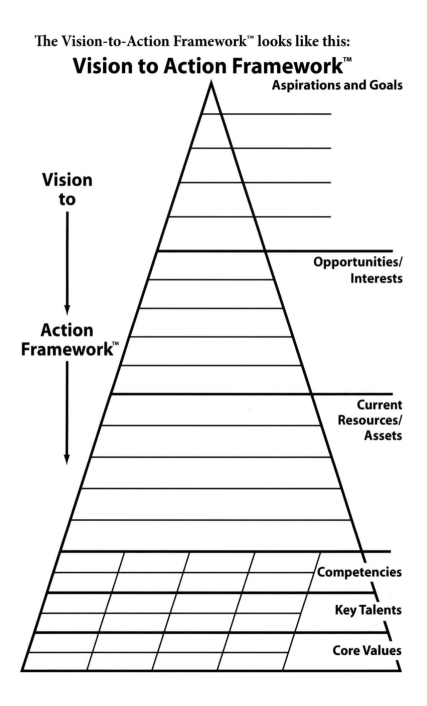

Aspirations and Goals

Vision to

Opportunities/ Interests

Action Framework™

Current Resources/ Assets

Competencies

Key Talents

Core Values

1. **Identify Aspirations and Goals, and Opportunities and Interests:**
   You will assess what is important to you from a broad perspective by examining your aspirations and goals. You will add those to the Vision-to-Action Framework™ and then look at your opportunities and interests as a basis for refining where you want to go in the future to achieve your goals. Moving your frame of reference from "what is" to "what could be" is key to action. You will examine your aspirations and goals and determine how well in alignment your identified opportunities are to those objectives. You will identify a broad set of opportunities and interests and then narrow them to the critical few that have the highest alignment to your aspirations and goals. You will then add those to the Vision-to-Action Framework™.

2. **Understand Your Resources:**
   Looking at your resources and assets is critical to determining your willingness and ability to execute against the opportunities you will identify. Wishfully thinking about opportunities and interests will not make them so. You must be willing and able to commit the resources and assets necessary to achieve those things. Along the way, you will identify potential pitfalls and safety steps along with your current resources and assets. You will add those to the Vision-to-Action Framework™.

3. **Recognize Your Importance:**
   Completion of the Vision-to-Action Framework™
   represents an important moment of recognition.
   You will have developed a picture of you based on
   values, talents and competencies and identified
   your aspirations and goals in the contexts of business and life. You will have identified opportunities
   and interests that align to those aspirations and
   goals and you will have specified certain resources
   and assets that you can bring to bear on achieving
   your objectives.

4. **Identify Your Critical Few Targets:**
   In the fourth step, you will more deeply delve into
   your opportunities and interests and develop specific actionable "targets." These targets represent
   very specific opportunities or interests that are
   defined and actionable. These "could-be" targets
   are something that you consider important and
   necessary to achieving your aspirations and goals.
   You will measure these targets against the elements
   of the Vision-to-Action Framework™ that you've
   already filled out and determine which ones offer
   the best alignment. At each step you will determine
   your willingness and ability to commit to the targets given the evaluation against the framework. If
   there are risks associated with the commitments,
   you will identify these.

The four models used in this section look like this:

Target Indentified to Opportunities/Interest™

OPPORTUNITIES

		Opportunity 1	Opportunity 2	Opportunity 3	Opportunity 4	Opportunity 5
TARGETS	Target 3					
	Target 2					
	Target 1					

Targets Mapped to Aspirations/Goals™

ASPIRATIONS/GOALS

		Aspirations/Goals 1	Aspirations/Goals 2	Aspirations/Goals 3	Aspirations/Goals 4	Aspirations/Goals 5
OPPORTUNITIES	Opportunity 1					
	Opportunity 2					
	Opportunity 3					
	Opportunity 4					
	Opportunity 5					

Competencies/Talents Identified to Top 5 Targets™

	Target 1	Target 2	Target 3	Target 4	Target 5
1. Leverage existing competencies and talents	Leverage	Leverage	Leverage	Leverage	Leverage
2. Broaden/deepen an existing competency	Add	Add	Add	Add	Add
3. Grow new or different competency	Grow	Grow	Grow	Grow	Grow
Risk: **Mitigation:**					

Top Targets Mapped to Resources Needed™

		Resource 1	Resource 2	Resource 3	New Resource Needed	Risk: Mitigation:
TOP TARGETS	Target 1					
	Target 2					
	Target 3					
	Target 4					
	Target 5					

6. **Blueprint Action Plan™ Development:**
In the final step, you will pull it all together in a Blueprint Action Plan™. You will be able to compare the Vision-to-Action Framework™ against the Blueprint Action Plan™ and see the level of integration you've achieved and the path you have set for yourself. You will have selected your critical few targets from a list of many and will see them in the Blueprint Action Plan™. You will have tested those targets and remained resolved to the priority of the few. You will also have recommitted several times to the targets you've set for yourself to ensure proper alignment with how you will execute against those targets. Finally, you will have identified an actionable plan for your targets and will have added them to the blueprint.

The Top 5 Targets/Top 3 Next Steps diagram looks like this:

Action Plan: Top 5 Targets/Top 3 Next Steps™
STEPS/TIMEFRAME

		Action Step 1	Step 1 Timeframe	Action Step 2	Step 2 Timeframe	Action Step 3	Step 3 Timeframe
TARGETS	Target 1						
	Target 2						
	Target 3						
	Target 4						
	Target 5						

The Blueprint Action Plan™ looks like this:

7. **Vision-to-Action:**
Once the next steps are completed you will be ready to get moving. You will be provided some guidance on how to get started, stay on track and track your progress.

So that's it in a nutshell. You are now ready to go to Chapter 1.

Blueprint Action Plan™

Aspirations					
Opportunities & Interests					
5 Top Targets	Target 1	Target 2	Target 3	Target 4	Target 5
Top 3 Comp/Talent Needed 1. Leverage					
2. Add					
3. Grow					
Top 3 Resources needed 1.					
2.					
3.					
First Next Step					
Timeframe					

Chapter 1

Taking Stock

The vision that you glorify in your mind, the ideal that you enthrone in your heart—this you will build your life by, and this you will become.
— James Allen, *As a Man Thinketh*

Starting with an assessment of your current situation is foundational to the entire exercise of this book. It may be clichéd to say it, but you cannot plan the person you want to be before understanding the person you are—your current values, talents and competencies.

In this chapter you'll be asked to first identify a broad set of characteristics in each category and then narrow them down to the critical few. You will select those values, talents and competencies that are your strongest assets and you'll begin to build the Vision-to-Action Framework™ from this selection. So let's get started.

Get Thinking

*For each Get Thinking section in the book I want you to remember that there are no wrong answers and that the process is one that you will repeat over time to keep it fresh and to reflect that your priorities and goals change in life.

What assets do you bring to the table? It seems like a simple question but these assets have several labels and each one is important to making quality choices. For each category of these assets—values, talents, competencies, aspirations/goals, opportunities/interests—you will do some brainstorming.

For each category there is a case study to further explain each asset. Included are some examples and some blank spaces for you to use when you come up with your own.

Try to think broadly and write freely in this Get Thinking section. The selections you make will help you begin to frame and understand where you are today. This is fundamental and you will want to take some time to do this. It is an important first step to understanding your starting point and what you can leverage.

In the Take Action section you will be asked to narrow to a critical few selections in each category. The lists that you create in the Get Thinking section will allow you to come back at certain points and ensure that you have made the "right" selections.

These are the six areas you will focus on. This evaluation becomes the basis of the Vision-to-Action Framework™. This single-page picture will be immensely helpful in understanding the key elements that will be the foundation of your blueprint.

1. Core values
2. Key talents
3. Current competencies
4. Aspirations and goals
5. Opportunities/interests
6. Current resources

Let's get to work.

Core Values

Core values represent aspects of your life that are most important to you. They are the foundation of how you interact with others every day. You may have a long list of values but the core values represent the "critical few" most important to you. Read the case study, then, using the examples provided, identify the values that are important to you.

Select as many values from the examples provided that apply to you and add others. Make sure that you can support each selected value with examples of how you have applied that value in your life. Circle as many values as you want, then check the eight that are most important to you and represent your core values.

Case Study

Jim is a fifteen-year veteran of a manufacturing company. His company is facing significant challenges and is restructuring. He joined the business right out of college and through hard work and commitment he has worked his way up to managing a team of fifty employees.

Jim is well-respected by his employees, having held many of the same positions his team members have. He respects his team, encourages communication through team meetings and coaches his employees to achieve their goals through teamwork and respect. Jim's boss appreciates his work ethic, down-to-earth work style and loyalty to the company. Jim understands his boss' need to ensure that work gets done in a timely manner and that his boss trusts his instincts and sense of independence, and he returns that appreciation with honesty and authenticity.

Key Learning

As you can see, Jim has a great deal to offer any work situation. A list of his core values might include hard work, perseverance, commitment, respect, open communication, teamwork and authenticity.

Equally as important, he has been able to demonstrate these values over a long period of time and these values are recognized by not only his boss but his employees as well. The importance of being able to identify values but also demonstrate situations in which they have been applied and recognized by others is critical. Values can transcend many work environments and should be an important consideration as well as a source of confidence when choosing additional goals and opportunities. The alignment of a solid base of values with well-chosen opportunities and interests can be the basis for continued success for Jim inside and outside of his company.

Circle or check the VALUES most important to you and add others in the space provided. Select the eight that are most important to you and represent your core values.

Humor	Directness	Partnership	Productivity
Service	Contribution	Excellence	Open-mindedness
Focus	Loyalty	Recognition	Harmony
Honest	Success	Accuracy	Accomplishment
Adventure	Fun	Tradition	Orderliness
Growth	Aesthetics	Inclusion	Recognition
Performance	Collaboration	Community	Being the best
Connection	Forward action	Lightness	Approachability

Freedom to choose	Acknowledgement	Camaraderie	Spirituality
Empowerment	Expressiveness	Integrity	Creativity
Independence	Nurturing	Joy	Beauty
Authenticity	Risk-taking	Peace	Elegance
Vitality	Trust	Fairness	Kindness
Sincerity	Transparent action	Sound judgment	Communication
Compassion	Equality	Optimism	Resiliency
Ambition	Balance	Self-control	Winning
Financial independence	Reliability	Change	Determination

_____   _____

_____   _____

_____   _____

_____   _____

_____   _____

_____   _____

_____   _____

Key Talents

Talents represent your natural abilities, strengths and superior personal characteristics. You are more than just competent in these areas; you are exceptional. These are your gifts, which you demonstrate readily with superior skill and ability. These abilities, strengths and superior personal characteristics are well-recognized by friends, family and colleagues.

These talents may also be hidden talents that others don't know well about you but that you do know. Read the case study first, then, using the examples provided, identify your talents. Select as many talents from the examples provided that apply to you and add others. Make sure you can support the talent with examples of how you have used or evidenced that talent. Once you have identified your talents, check eight that are your key talents.

Case Study

Sandra is a tenured high school teacher with ten years of experience. She is a gifted music teacher in both her accomplished ability as a pianist as well as her love of teaching. Her ability to relate to students and their various learning styles while helping them excel at their learning is well-known throughout the school.

Sandra's kindness is exemplary and her dedication to her students has won her recognition many times over the years. She is focused on student achievement and helping students learn to their fullest abilities in their own personal ways. She is particularly poised in her ability to demonstrate her capability at the piano and also thoughtful in showing the students several different ways to master and develop their talents. She is admired by her peers as well and often sought after for advice.

Key Learning

Sandra is gifted in teaching music, an accomplished pianist, inspiring to students, exceptionally kind and dedicated, outwardly focused on helping students excel, poised in her presence and thoughtful.

She has dedicated herself to the classroom environment but could possibly define other opportunities to leverage her talents.

While she may be very satisfied to stay in the classroom environment for the foreseeable future she certainly can be confident that other opportunities would not be hard to define. It would be entirely possible that she could leverage her talents to reach many students beyond the traditional classroom. Sandra also could find opportunities consulting with other teachers on teaching methods and encouraging the success of students.

Circle or check the talents that apply to you and add others. Then check eight that are your key talents:

Sound judgment	Continuous learner	Problem-solver
Communicator	Influencer	Flexible
Initiative	Self-confident	Teamwork
Creative	Innovative	Adaptable
Strategic thinker	Skillful manager	Resourceful
Responsiveness	Planner	Organized
Detail-oriented	Designer of solutions	Goal-oriented
Forward-thinking	Result-oriented	Superior leader
Business acumen	Client focus	Disciplined
Poised	Resilient	Thorough
Thoughtful	Mature	Kind
Fair	Inclusive	Persuasive

Hard-working	Decisive	Aggressive
Respectful	Practical	Calm in crisis
Honest	Broad perspective	Professional
Team leader	Analytical	Listener
Improvement-focused	Motivational	Relationship-builder

_____   _____

_____   _____

_____   _____

_____   _____

_____   _____

_____   _____

Current Competencies

Competencies are learned abilities or capabilities. While thinking about your competencies, focus less on your natural abilities and key talents from the previous sections. Think more about those capabilities you have learned and can demonstrate proficiently.

Many of these competencies may come from the list you just completed but did not identify as key talents. Taking stock of your competencies is extremely important because when combined with your key talents, they paint a picture of your strengths and what you bring to the table. This will not only help you build a holistic perspective of yourself but will help you later on as you evaluate your choices and begin to contemplate opportunities and interests that require leveraging existing key talents and competencies.

It will also help you in identifying new competencies necessary to achieve your goals. Read the case study first, then think of the competencies that you have learned and applied in the jobs you have held or areas in which you have excelled. Make sure that you can support the competencies you list with examples of how you have used each one.

> *Hint: You can leverage the work you just completed in the Key Talents section. Review your list of key talents on this page, then cross out the eight key talents you chose and bring forward the remaining ones as competencies.*

Case Study

Allen is a supervisor for an insurance company. His company is downsizing amid financial pressures. He has been with the company for five years and he keeps his team focused and organized on meeting the goals expected by the company. He is good at staying flexible and being prepared to rally the team to unexpected challenges. His customer satisfaction scores are above average and he is known for his fairness in resolving issues.

Allen is hard-working and expects the same of his team in order to ensure that budgets are met and case resolutions are within goal. He is thoughtful and respectful of his employees and provides them with good communication on departmental changes, procedure changes and company news. His employees like and respect him and appreciate his inclusive style.

Key Learning

Allen is team-focused, organized, goal-oriented, flexible, customer-focused, fair, hard-working, budget-minded, motivated for both results and productivity and a good communicator. These are attributes that can be counted as talents if Allen is particularly good at them, but they also stand up as competencies because achieving proficiency in these areas requires learning and practicing new behaviors.

These are great competencies to have regardless of work environment. He is still young in his career and may be able to identify several of these competencies that he wants to develop and grow into talents. Regardless, he should continue to strive for repeatedly demonstrating these competencies. He would be a steady contributor in any environment and well-liked by many people.

Review and identify additional competencies you may have from the list below and then narrow that list to eight key competencies and circle or check those.

Sound judgment	Continuous learner	Problem-solver
Communicator	Influencer	Flexible
Initiative	Self-confident	Teamwork
Creative	Innovative	Adaptable
Strategic thinker	Skillful manager	Resourceful
Responsiveness	Planner	Organized
Detail-oriented	Designer of solutions	Goal-oriented
Forward-thinking	Result-oriented	Superior leader

Business acumen	Client focus	Disciplined
Poised	Resilient	Thorough
Thoughtful	Mature	Kind
Fair	Inclusive	Persuasive
Hard-working	Decisive	Aggressive
Respectful	Practical	Calm in crisis
Honest	Broad perspective	Professional
Team leader	Analytical	Listener
Improvement-focused	Motivational	Relationship builder

_____   _____

_____   _____

_____   _____

_____   _____

_____   _____

_____   _____

_____   _____

Aspirations and Goals

Aspirations and goals are what drive you. They are the big important things in your life that guide the decisions you make as you strive to achieve them. While the terms may sound similar in nature, goals are more specific than aspirations and are more concrete representations of how you might achieve your aspirations.

Aspirations and goals should give you a sense of purpose and meaning. Many aspirations and goals focus on what you want for yourself, your family, your career and your life. They are not likely to change in the short-term like opportunities and interests do. Your aspirations and goals are not about which car you want to own. These are about the person you want to become.

Aspirations are long-term in nature and represent points in the future you want to work toward. This is an important distinction since in the next section you will be asked to identify opportunities and interests. The opportunities you identify there will represent what you may work on to achieve the aspiration or goals stated here. Read the case study, think about what is important to you, what you value and what you want to strive for in the future. Jot down some notes. It may be helpful to start each aspiration or goal with, "I aspire to" or, "It is important to me" or, "I want" or, "My goal is."

Here are a few examples of what you might list as your goals and aspirations: I want to be in perfect health; I want to be happy in personal and career relationships; I want to utilize my skills and talents in a career that challenges me and offers fulfillment.

Case Study

Maria is an assistant at a childcare facility where she has worked for eight years, beginning immediately after high school. The company is closing the location at which she works. She has a true love of children and teaching new things whether about nature or art or reading and writing.

Maria has begun to think about going back to school, at either a vocational school or community college, to become a teacher. She hopes someday to marry and would like a family of her own.

She also would like to own her own daycare facility. Maria has a lot of ideas about how to make her own business a truly wonderful learning experience for children. She knows that starting her own business will take more money than she has, so each week she is putting aside a small amount in the hopes that someday she will be able to realize this dream.

Maria has even begun to think of other creative ways she could make additional money. She has contemplated writing a children's book and even tutoring. She has also thought about organizing some field trips for the kids on weekends. While she thinks about how many children she could make a difference for she is concerned with the immediate prospect that she may not be able to transfer to another facility location.

Key Learning

Maria should be commended for her clarity of goals and aspirations. She wants to become a teacher, marry, have a family, own her own business, save money for later, creatively make money and make a difference for children. These goals, like yours, should be the bases for countless opportunities and targets that Maria could identify in pursuing a path toward what she ultimately wants.

The opportunities and targets that she will identify should support, align with and assist in the attainment of her aspirations and goals. Alignment is key in making sure that Maria's actions today are designed for achieving her aspirations and goals, no matter how far away they may be.

She may be well-advised to prioritize her goals so that she can more clearly identify opportunities and targets based on these priorities with a focus on immediacy. She will want to ensure that she is using her resources wisely on the highest-priority targets. This prioritization of goals may take a couple of tries but will be well worth the work and ensure that she is making the highest and best use of her time.

Identify as many aspirations and goals as you can and then narrow them down to five, and circle or check those. It might be helpful to think of your aspirations and goals in the following categories: health, wealth/money, knowledge, love, family, business/career, serving/giving back.

Opportunities/Interests

Identifying opportunities and interests will help to clarify your aspirations and goals and will begin to help you get clear about where you want to spend your effort. They may be work-related or non-work-related. You may already be working on some of these areas.

Most importantly, these are general areas of opportunity and interest that you believe would align you to your goals and aspirations and on which you would be willing to expend your resources. At this point, the opportunities and interests you identify will likely be general. That's ok. They are intended to be general at this point. They may be areas like health care, finance, banking, education, consulting, writing/authoring, product development, sales, engineering, interior design, landscape management, property management, volunteering, cooking, domestic services, retail, technology or teaching.

What you're focusing on right now are areas of interest, not a specific job. But even though you are not specifically identifying a job, you must be clear about the reason you have an interest in a given area and describe how it aligns to your aspirations and goals.

Ultimately, you must be willing to spend your time, money and other resources on these things because these opportunities are meaningful to you. This is your personal satisfaction list. Spending time on these opportunities and interests helps you feel happier, more fulfilled and satisfied every day. You may want to set aside time to focus on identifying your opportunities and interests list as it is critical to the rest of the work. It is also important to see the alignment with your goals and aspirations.

If an opportunity or interest is not aligned in some way to your aspirations and goals it may not be a good candidate. It may be better as a hobby. It may be helpful to start each opportunity or interest with, "To advance my aspirations and goals, I would like to..."

Case Study

Kevin is a college graduate who majored in marketing. He has not been able to find work in his chosen field of sports marketing. Although he knows his goals are to make a lot of money and to work for himself, he is very concerned that he may never be able to find a job in his field.

Kevin has been working at a local department store while trying to find work and he is hard-working. He'd applied himself while in college and graduated with a 3.0 GPA. He is willing to work hard to reach his goals but thinks he should consider alternatives.

An avid gamer, he has thought he could improve several of the computer games he has become expert at playing. He'd taken several computer science courses in college and has thought that he would be good at selling computer game concepts to companies, leveraging knowledge from his marketing courses. In the meantime, he wants to pick up a part-time job at the local automotive repair shop, and so he can learn to work on his car. He knows everything about his car and thinks he would be good at repairing and servicing other people's cars as well. Having known the man who owns the repair shop for years, he may even be able to fix up one of the old cars at the shop and sell it to help pay for living expenses.

Key Learning

Kevin has many opportunities to examine. He would like to improve or invent computer games, sell computer games, build his skills through automotive repair, service other people's cars and sell cars. This diversity of interests can lead him to many opportunities so he will want to prioritize these opportunities carefully. In addition, he will have to prioritize his time while working to have enough to spend in a worthwhile way exploring these opportunities in depth. It's also likely that some of Kevin's opportunities will require financial and material resources and that is why prioritizing opportunities is so important. That being said, the breadth of these opportunities will provide him with a broad set of choices that are well-worth the effort.

Identify the areas of opportunity and interest that you have and narrow the list to the top five, and circle or check those.

Health care	Finance	Banking
Education	Consult	Writing/Authoring
Product development	Sales	Engineering
Interior design	Social services	Food service
Accounting	Automotive	Business development
Manufacturing	Technology	Real estate
Catering	Law enforcement	Advertising
Broadcasting	Journalism	Coaching

_____   _____

_____   _____

_____   _____

_____   _____

_____   _____

_____   _____

_____   _____

Current Resources

Looking at your resources and assets is critical to determining your willingness and ability to execute against the opportunities you've identified. These resources and assets can be monetary and non-monetary. Sometimes the hardest resources to commit to are the non-monetary ones, like time and effort for research or fact-finding.

Wishfully thinking about opportunities and interests will not make them so. You must be willing and able to commit the resources and assets necessary to achieve those things with reason. Equally dangerous is over-committing to resources or assets, putting yourself or your family in a bad situation. So, along the way, we will make sure you identify potential pitfalls and safety steps.

Current resources can include those people and things you can leverage to help get things done: friends, family colleagues and role models. You have them all around you—people you know who will help you when asked or who you can learn from by reading about them or observing them. The obvious resources are money or time available to spend working on your opportunities and interests. These are assets that can be called upon and leveraged as you work on your opportunities and interests.

Case Study

Steve owns his own company and has built quite a reputation for himself over thirty years as an honest, hard-working expert at home remodeling. Although his company is not big he has never been without work and keeps a small team of dedicated professionals like himself.

Steve thought he would be able to sell his business to an interested company but most of the larger companies in his area have fallen on hard times. Having failed to find a buyer, he has decided to expand his business but he knows this will take some hard work.

Although his employees are dedicated and loyal, finding others of equal caliber has always been hard. He does think some referrals could come from his employees but he would have to expand his shop to accommodate the needed increase in physical workspace.

His shop would have to be moved as part of the expansion and that would cost time and money. While he can see his company growing, he wants to be conservative in just how much of each he is willing to invest. He does not want to impact his current sales projections and is already working over forty hours a week. Finally, he needs to estimate the increase in sales he could expect so that he knows how much he would need to expand. He thinks there are several business Web sites that might have information that can help.

Key Learning

Steve will definitely benefit from understanding his resource requirements. His high standards are evidenced in the reputation he has built for himself and the caliber of employee he has working for him today. He would do well to get referrals from his employees as they understand his work ethic and he will want to understand the commitment needed to expand to a bigger shop—the bigger shop's expenses and the time required to move to the new shop.

The Internet may help secure the needed market information to estimate how to increase sales, but he will have to determine how to mitigate the risk of impacting existing sales and burning himself out. He has his work cut out for him and will need to think carefully about these choices.

Identify as many of your current resources as you can and then narrow them down to the top five, and circle or check those.

| People in my network | Internet for research and knowledge | People experienced in the area of interest |
| Professional advisors | Savings | Time available |

_____   _____

_____   _____

_____   _____

_____   _____

_____   _____

_____   _____

_____   _____

Take Action

Now you can build your personal Vision-to-Action Framework™. This point in the book represents the most important component in the foundation for your Blueprint Action Plan™, which is completing your Vision-to-Action Framework™. By doing this you will have painted a picture of YOU and where you are today.

Select the **Vision-to-Action Framework**™ (Fig 1.) from the back of the book. It looks like this:

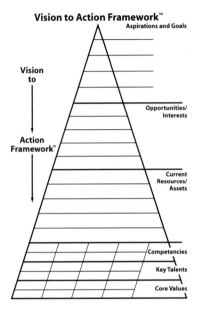

This frame will become the basis for the deeper examination of your choices so it is important that you think about each step. In the Get Thinking section you brainstormed each category and made some choices. You also narrowed your identification to five or eight elements that were the most important to you.

Recheck the lists you developed in the Get Thinking section for each category and validate the selections you made. This validation is intended to challenge you to get to the critical few things that will make a difference for you.

Your Core Values: From the Get Thinking section, validate and select the eight core values that are most important to you. These are non-negotiable and are the foundation for many decisions you make on a day-to-day basis even though you might not be consciously aware of it. List these eight core values on the Vision-to-Action Framework™.

Key Talents: From the Get Thinking section, validate and select the eight key talents that best describe your natural abilities. These key talents are easily recognized and represent a key advantage for you in life or in your career. List these eight key talents on the Vision-to-Action Framework™.

Your Current Competencies: From the Get Thinking section, validate and select the eight competencies that best characterize you today. These are eight competencies that stand the test of time and that others recognize in you as well. List these eight competencies on the Vision-to-Action Framework™.

Aspirations and Goals: From the Get Thinking section, validate and select the five aspirations and goals that are most important to you right now. List these aspirations and goals on the Vision-to-Action Framework™.

Opportunities/Interests: From the Get Thinking section, validate and select the five opportunities/interests that are priorities for you today and that resonate most. List these opportunities and interests on the Vision-to-Action Framework™.

Resources: From the Get Thinking section, validate and select the five current resources that best represent your pool of assets. List these on the Vision-to-Action Framework™.

Congratulations. You have just completed your Vision-to-Action Framework™. This is the most important component in building the foundation for your blueprint. It will provide the context for the remaining steps and for the choices you will make. It is a living document, so you can revise it if you feel you can make better choices as you look at the big picture of your life. You will want to update this over time as well because as your goals are accomplished or your desires change, the Vision-to-Action Framework™ can work for you and become part of your decision-making process going forward.

Chapter 1 Summary

The completion of Chapter 1 represents a significant accomplishment. You have identified, examined, contemplated and selected the most important components that frame you: your values, competencies and talents, aspirations and goals, opportunities and interests, and resources.

Most importantly, you have provided yourself with a strong foundation in identifying your values, competencies and talents that will be used over and over again in assessing your future opportunities. You are able to understand the alignment between these foundational elements and your goals and aspirations. You have identified your aspirations and goals in a "big picture" way that will take you beyond tomorrow or next week or next month. These cornerstone activities form the basis of the Vision-to-Action Framework™.

You have also framed your opportunities and interests in a broad, general way in five different areas, and you have identified your resources in order to understand what you can leverage against your opportunities. These two components will allow you to begin to see more clearly the choices necessary to get from vision to action. In the next chapters, you will evaluate many detailed opportunities against your Vision-to-Action Framework™ and further see the breadth of opportunity before you. Through continued evaluation you will make informed, well-thought-out choices.

This is a significant point of reflection and understanding. It also represents a tremendous advantage for you in any economic or work environment. Your ability to articulate your goals and the kinds of opportunities you are interested in is an important aspect in being able to seek successful work that allows you to work both productively and in alignment with the elements that will help you be most successful.

In this tough economic climate the hard work you have put in will be well worth it. Your ability to clearly demonstrate your values, competencies and talents represents a differentiation point that offers a competitive advantage. Combined with your clarity of aspirations, goals and opportunities, you are well-prepared to demonstrate your knowledge and understanding of where you would be most successful and why. With just this first step you are better-armed and prepared to compete and succeed.

Chapter 2

Opportunities and Targets

Become a possibilitarian. No matter how dark things seem to be or actually are, raise your sights and see possibilities—always see them for they are always there.

—Norman Vincent Peale

Get Thinking

The opportunities specified so far are general and have provided the context needed to put together your Vision-to-Action Framework™. Those opportunities need greater definition and specificity to become actionable. In this chapter you will define targets for each opportunity.

Think of a target just as you would one at a shooting range or an amusement park. The target represents your specific area of focus. Look at the Vision-to-Action Framework™, think about each opportunity and explore the possible specific actions or work or jobs within each category. These are the things on which you can actually focus.

You will want to identify the kinds of things within each category that you would find exciting or that you are passionate about or that you want to explore the possibilities of.

For each opportunity/interest you will want to identify several targets within that category so that you will be able to compare and contrast the differences. Don't worry about how you will accomplish each target; that process will be explored later on. For now just focus on specifically identifying what you would like to do or focus on. You may find it useful to think about the best job or best personal experience you have had in the last few years. What were the characteristics of this job or personal experience that you specifically liked and how would this translate into a specific target?

Case Study

Tom has spent thirty-five years in the banking industry. Tom is considering retirement but wants to evaluate the possibility of staying part-time with the company for a while as he decides whether or not to retire fully.

Tom knows he has several opportunities in the area of consulting that would leverage his deep banking background. He may be able to find a large, corporate firm or smaller, local firm that is looking for part-time consultants. Tom has also considered striking out on his own, consulting independently, leveraging the many contacts he has developed over the years.

Tom's other interest is teaching and he has volunteered for many years as a mentor for small business owners, and has grown to love the opportunity to impart some of his knowledge to very appreciative owners. He thinks he may know several small companies that could use some help and would be willing to pay him.

Another opportunity is writing. He may be able to write articles for some of the small business magazines, but would need to determine which ones as there are many. He also wants to look at teaching in a classroom environment and has some contacts at the local college.

Key Learning

Tom has several opportunities to consult, teach and write. These opportunities will allow him to develop several targets within each category of opportunity. His list of targets are large, corporate consulting, small, local consulting firms and independent consulting.

Tom believes he has several targets in the area of teaching and may be able to teach business principles to small businesses or write articles for several small business magazines. He may also be able to teach on the college level. A fuller exploration of these targets will allow him to understand the commitments he must make to be successful as well as the time and money he may have to invest. He may also identify additional targets in the process, allowing him to choose from a broad range of alternatives.

Refer to your list of opportunities and interests and then list and brainstorm as many targets of action as you can think of.

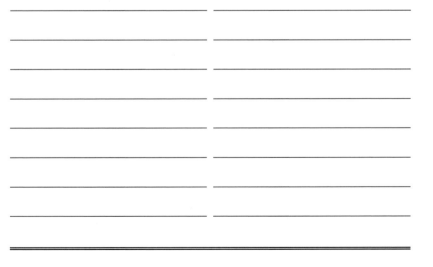

Take Action

Step 1: Select the **Targets Identified to Opportunities** matrix (Fig. 2) from the back of the book. It looks like this:

Target Indentified to Opportunities/Interest™

		Opportunity 1	Opportunity 2	Opportunity 3	Opportunity 4	Opportunity 5
	Target 3					
	Target 2					
	Target 1					

(left label: TARGETS) (top label: OPPORTUNITIES)

Step 2: Using the Vision-to-Action Framework™ (Fig. 1), list your opportunities/interests across the top of the matrix.

Step 3: From the Get Thinking section, select three targets for each opportunity/interest and enter them in the matrix.

Step 4: Contemplate the targets. Eliminate redundancies (if you have listed that you want to be an author and that you want to write a book, then you can combine the two). Test for specificity. Ensure that they resonate with you as areas on which you are willing to spend your time working .

Step 5: Test for satisfaction. If any one of these target opportunities were a reality for you today, would you be excited enough to work on it every day, based on what you know right now? Don't assume that you know everything or pressure yourself to know all the facts today. There will be time later to evaluate what you need.

Chapter 2 Summary

The completion of Chapter 2 has brought you one step closer to realizing your goals. Your ability to see the possibilities that each opportunity represents is an important part of expanding your choices and enhancing your ability to succeed. You can see the importance of categorizing targets against the opportunities in order see more clearly all possibilities. This structure and process will allow you to better understand the fit of the targets with your opportunities and, as you continue to identify targets, will help you focus on the best targets. If you have had difficulty identifying three targets for each opportunity, that's ok. The act of thinking about targets will continue as you build out your Blueprint Action Plan™. You can come back to this point as you identify new targets and want to evaluate them.

As you saw in the case study, looking at your background, your experiences and the competencies and talents that you can leverage is a good place to start. Looking at your network and the people you know can be a source of new ideas and brainstorming of targets. Ask a friend or colleague or family member for ideas about targets and at what you are good or talented. Not every target will work out and that is ok too. The creative process of identifying targets is the most important part of the work and having a robust list of possibilities will give you a greater chance of making the best choices.

This exercise is an important step in allowing you to better understand what is possible. Being able to imagine those possibilities will allow you to see options you didn't think were there and will allow you to be more hopeful about the future. You will also see that you don't need to get overly focused or invested in one target.

Many targets provide you with options. Staying flexible and seeing many possibilities without jumping to a conclusion is most important here. In a tough economic climate the more targets you can envision, the better your chances of success. Even if a target does not represent an ideal possibility it may move you closer to your goals. In the next chapter you will align those targets to your goals and aspirations in order to keep yourself on track and allow yourself to make the best choices from the many possibilities.

Chapter 3

Alignment Matters

Man is a goal seeking animal. His life only has meaning if he is reaching out and striving for his goals.

—Aristotle

Get Thinking

Now that you know more about your opportunities/interests and targets, let's look at how these align to your aspirations and goals. The result of this part of the work will allow you to see the fit of your targets with your aspirations and goals.

Remember: Some targets could fit under several aspirations and goals. Others may not be perfect fits. You are looking to make this alignment the best possible way, knowing that there may not be perfect choices. What it will allow you to do is think about the targets you have identified and how they are aligning to your aspirations and goals and whether these targets are useful and worthwhile in that context.

The targets you have identified may or may not further your aspirations and goals. With this knowledge you can choose to rethink and refine your targets. You always have the option to rethink and refine any part of the work you have completed until you are satisfied with the outcome. There are no wrong answers!

Case Study

Janet has a great sense of her goals. She graduated college with an interior design degree and has achieved success in the five years since, in both independently consulting with clients as well as working for one of the top design firms in town. The ability to work for both herself and the design firm has been a significant source of satisfaction.

However, Janet wants to focus on several new opportunities to continue to diversify and expand her personal brand. She would like to develop a line of home products, perhaps write a book on interior design and partner with another designer in order to expand her base of clients. She needs to think carefully about these opportunities and the targets that each one them will present. She will need to decide the types of home products and the best way to get those products to market either independently or through her firm.

Janet may have another alternative as well, which is to partner with a manufacturing company specializing in home products. She will need to identify the type of interior design book she wants to write and decide if she wants to collaborate with someone to write it. Expanding her client base can be done in numerous ways and she will need to think about that as well.

Once these targets are more fully defined, aligning them to the best fit with her goals will allow her to think about the implications of each, which will lead to more informed choices.

Key Learning

Janet has two primary goals: to continue working for herself as an independent consultant and to continue working with the design firm, even if on a reduced schedule. Her opportunities are to develop home products, write a book and expand her clients. She may be able to partner with someone for each of these opportunities or attempt them on her own. Janet will want to specify for each of these opportunities the specific home products or book type or client type that she is targeting. The exploration of each of these targets in combination with the opportunities will allow her to develop a robust sense of her targets and more fully understand her choices. She may also uncover additional opportunities or targets in the course. Aligning these, then, to her goals of continuing to work independently or with the design firm will allow her to more fully understand the implications of each decision and how the degree to which those targets support her goals.

Take Action

Step 1: Select the **Targets Mapped to Aspirations and Goals** matrix (Fig. 3) from the back of the book. It looks like this:

Step 2: Using the Vision-to-Action Framework™ (Fig. 1), list your opportunities/interests vertically down the matrix. Using the Vision-to-Action Framework™, list your aspirations and goals across the top of the matrix.

Step 3: Using the Targets Identified to Opportunities matrix (Fig. 2) completed in Chapter 2, select a target that you have identified and map it to the best fit under the Aspirations/Goals column. Each target may have several places where it could fit. Choose the one that best fits with your aspirations and goals.

Step 4: For each row of opportunities, prioritize the three targets based on your level of interest. What would you be most interested in working on right now? You should have enough interest and energy to want to start working on those things right away. Don't worry about the how; just think about the now. When finished, for each row of opportunities/interests, you will have prioritized your three targets.

Step 5: Now go to each Opportunities row and select the targets you've prioritized as most important. Circle or highlight these.

Step 6: Look at the selected targets in the context of the Vision-to-Action Framework™. Do these targets still resonate in the context of that picture? Are the priorities right in the context of your goals and aspirations and other opportunities and targets? Are you able to see yourself making the commitment to work on these targets? If you answered "no" to any of these questions, rethink the value of the selected target and make a change.

Chapter 3 Summary

The completion of Chapter 3 is the most important step in expanding your understanding of alignment and its importance. Your ability be closely aligned to your aspirations and goals will give you a greater sense of satisfaction and accomplishment. This sense of satisfaction and accomplishment can lead to a greater chance of overall success.

You also saw that targets can align to more than one goal and that thinking about the implications of this is valuable and helpful to understanding the target. Well-thought-out targets aligned with well-thought-out goals are a powerful combination leading to greater success. If you had difficulty aligning a target to a goal, thinking through the implications of each alignment is a good way to find the best fit. It may be that there is not a perfect fit and in this case understanding the implications of the alignment of a target to a goal will help you choose the best possible combination.

As you saw in the case study, looking at the various combinations of targets with goals may allow you to develop a more robust sense of the targets, more fully define them and understand the choices to be made. This understanding may lead to additional targets or opportunity identification in the future. It is through these insights that the right combination of opportunities and targets will emerge.

This exercise is an important part of the process in allowing you to freely explore your opportunities and targets without recourse or regret. It is an exercise in open exploration and should be considered a place where **there are no wrong answers.** It is a creative exercise designed to allow you to experiment with the concept of alignment and just how powerful it can be in attaining your goals in a fully supportive way.

In the next chapter you will determine which competencies and talents to use to achieve each target. You will be acting with certainty knowing that your efforts will be enhanced as a result of fully appreciating these aligned choices.

Chapter 4

Leverage, Add
and Grow

*It is time for us to stand and cheer for the doer, the
achiever, the one who recognizes the challenge and
does something about it.*

—Vince Lombardi

Get Thinking

This chapter will help you understand what competencies
you will need to be successful as you pursue your targets.
It is important to know that your current competencies
and talents represent a tremendous advantage in achieving the targets you have chosen. When properly selected, opportunities and
targets are aligned with competencies and talents that can be successfully leveraged against those objectives. The combination is the
basis for realizing your aspirations and goals.

Equally important is recognizing that you need to grow or
deepen certain competencies in order to be successful with a target. You must be prepared and willing to add new competencies
when they are critical to achieving a target you've selected. Some

new competencies may be complementary to a competency or talent you already have. In this case the effort to strengthen what you need may be minimal.

Other needed competencies may represent a deepening or broadening of a skill or capability. This may require a moderate investment of your time and energy. In other instances you may have to develop a new competency. In that case you may have to build knowledge of that area first before you can successfully execute against the target. This path could take you a while and you will have to assess your willingness and ability to learn and to invest the time and possibly money to gain the needed knowledge and understanding.

This difference—understanding what you already have, what you must broaden or deepen and what you must build new—is critical to understanding and recognizing what it will take to achieve a target. You will have to think about this carefully and make clear, sound choices.

Case Study

Robert is a seasoned veteran of the residential real estate business. He has been selling real estate for twenty-five years. The real estate agency Robert works for has been hard hit by the current economic conditions so he must explore his options. He has determined that one of his opportunities is to write a newsletter for prospective clients, to keep them posted on the most current real estate news and timely advice. He wants to be able to reach a variety of home buyers and offer specialty advice to these clients through specific articles in the newsletter. Robert believes this will help keep him known in the community and plugged into the business and maybe able to generate additional leads for both selling and listing as the market turns around. Robert does see some challenges in getting the newsletter up and running. He can leverage his broad knowledge of the real estate industry in identifying many different interesting article topics and he has written hundreds of marketing pieces for properties over the years. However, he knows he may have to brush up on his writing skills for this type of newsletter. In addition, he does not have any graphic design experience or publication experience of this kind. He does not think he wants to invest his time in learning these new skills and he does see the risk of jumping too quickly into this venture before knowing the cost. He believes he needs to research the opportunity first.

Key Learning

Robert certainly has several competencies he can leverage in the development of his newsletter opportunity. He has deep knowledge of the residential real estate business that can be leveraged and he has written marketing materials for individual properties. He knows the market and will be able to leverage this competency to identify topics of interest. But Robert will likely have to add additional capabilities to his current assets to make the opportunity work. He will likely have to study and learn about writing styles for newsletters and it's not clear yet what this will take and how much time and money might be required. Robert does know he will have to invest money in securing the graphic design help and publication capability he'll need. The cost of both will have to be considered carefully to ensure success.

Take Action

Step 1: Select the **Competencies/Talents Identified to Top 5 Targets** matrix (Fig. 4) from the back of the book. It looks like this:

Competencies/Talents Identified to Top 5 Targets™

	Target 1	Target 2	Target 3	Target 4	Target 5
1. Leverage existing competencies and talents	Leverage	Leverage	Leverage	Leverage	Leverage
2. Broaden/deepen an existing competency	Add	Add	Add	Add	Add
3. Grow new or different competency	Grow	Grow	Grow	Grow	Grow
Risk: **Mitigation:**					

Step 2: Across the top of the matrix list your top five number-one targets identified in the previous chapter.

Step 3: For each target, look at competency number one. Look at the competencies and talents listed on the Vision-to-Action Framework™. Identify a competency or talent you already have that can be leveraged to achieve the target. If you do not have any competencies or talents in the targeted area leave that blank. More on this later.

Step 4: For each target, look at competency number two. A complementary competency is one in which you already have some proficiency and only requires you to deepen or broaden your knowledge in that area. It is NOT a new or different skill or capability. For each target identify a competency that must be expanded in order to achieve the target. If you do not have a competency that can be deepened or broadened to achieve the target leave that blank. More on this later.

Step 5: For each target, look at competency number three. Identify a new skill or capability that will be needed to achieve the target. In a case where you have a target and have not been able to identify a current competency or a complementary competency, identify that you must grow your knowledge in this area in order to be successful. This does not mean that you cannot achieve the target. However, recognition that you must grow your knowledge of a particular area will help you identify the right resources and action plans in the following chapters.

Step 6: Look at the competencies for each target. Are there risks in achieving the target with the competencies/talents you have identified? State what the risk is in the last row for each target. Identify an action you can take to minimize the effect of the risk.

Step 7: Look at the **Targets Mapped to Aspirations and Goals** matrix (Fig. 3). Look at the **Competencies Identified to Top 5 targets** matrix (Fig. 4). Evaluate your selection of targets. Think about the competencies needed. Determine your willingness and ability to invest in building competencies you need and don't have. Evaluate the risks and actionable steps you can take to minimize these risks. Revise if necessary.

Chapter 4 Summary

The completion of Chapter 4 has reinforced the importance of the hard work you did in identifying your competencies and talents. Those sixteen competencies and talents can now be brought to bear on the attainment of your targets and the successful accomplishment of your goals. The ability to select from your existing competencies and talents has shown you very specifically where you have your greatest leverage. Identifying where you must add depth and breadth to existing competencies should have helped you see where there will be some work and identifying where you must grow new competencies should have pointed you to your greatest challenge and most thoughtful consideration. The identification of risks and mitigation plans should crystallize this for you and help you contemplate your willingness to commit to the target.

The case study should have shown you the value of identifying competencies and talents that you can leverage but also the importance of contemplating the full complement of competencies that are needed. Time, money and resources will be needed to fill the gaps that are created when you do not fully match well with a target. Recognizing this, as in the case study, will help you evaluate the extent to which you are willing to commit resources to broadening or deepening those competencies or having to build new.

This exercise is an important recognition of what you bring to the table in both competencies and talents. It is a cause for celebration that every single person has something to offer and when matched with the right opportunity and target can be a very powerful and successful result. But serious contemplation is necessary in order to ensure good choices and the best selection of targets in combination with competencies. It's not easy to build new competencies where none exist. It also may be an entirely worthwhile endeavor to do just that if it means pursuing a target that has great alignment to your aspirations and goals.

Chapter 5

Marshal Your Resources

The expectations of life depend on diligence; the mechanic that would perfect his work must first sharpen his tools.

—Confucius

Get Thinking

What arsenal of resources do you have that you can bring to bear on realizing your targets? This is an important consideration and must be contemplated before pursuing any opportunity or target. It is well worth the time and effort now to evaluate this aspect before you get started. It may save you a costly learning experience down the line.

First and foremost are people; people in your network, people who know those people, professional advisors, colleagues, friends and family members are all potentially your best resources. People are your strongest allies here and may be your least costly assets.

Second-most important is time. Time needed to work on the opportunities and targets you have selected and the willingness and commitment needed to do so. This can be more difficult as the opportunities and targets become more complex and/or your personal situation doesn't provide the required time. Think about how many hours a day or week you can set aside to work on your targets of opportunity. This time element may represent vacation days spent working on your target, or even weekends and holidays. Jot down in the space provided below minimum and maximum time a week you think you will be willing and able to spend in total working on your targets. This time will have to be allocated across all targets.

A third resource needed is money. You will want to think about the amount of money you are willing to invest in any target of opportunity to get started and at what point you will say, "No more." Using the space below, write down the minimum and maximum amount of money you are willing to sink into your targets. These amounts may represent what you have in savings that you would be willing to spend or what you are willing to take out of your paycheck.

I mentioned in the introduction that you must contemplate your willingness and ability to commit resources to your targets. It's worth mentioning here again the importance of understanding the commitment and risk associated with committing those resources. Be willing to commit! But use caution here. Over-committing resources can put you or your family in a bad situation, so think about the balance between resources and risk and be sure that it is reasonable.

Time: Willing to commit: Min _____ Max _____

Money: Willing to commit: Min _____ Max _____

Case Study

Amy is a talented artist working for a small art studio. She graduated with top honors from college and quickly established herself as one of the best artists in town. However, the studio has fallen on hard times and the owners have decided to close it. She has done well there for three years but knows she will now have to go out on her own and establish her own studio to have a place to work on her art and showcase her work. She has saved enough money to pay for a small, two-room studio for a year but she wants to ensure that she picks the right location to maintain exposure for her work.

Amy will need a top real estate agent to help her, and she also wants to start getting the word out that she is starting her own studio. She has a good relationship with the current owners of the studio and they have offered to help her with connections. She also wants to establish a certain look and feel about the studio in order to create a wonderful experience for her customers and a better understanding of her work. She is willing to spend her free time researching this to determine what that look and feel should be.

Key Learning

Amy wants to be more independent as an artist. She has a identified a great opportunity in establishing her own studio. She will want to carefully consider her resources as she will be solely responsible for her choices and in this economic climate she will want to make prudent choices. The location Amy chooses will have to be carefully evaluated and she will want to examine the cost considerations associated with each possible location. A real estate agent could certainly help. Getting the word out at the right time will be paramount to generating traffic quickly and she should consider several alternative methods both through the connections mentioned as well as other alternatives. She will have to invest time and money in establishing the look and feel she wants and in addition to understanding the choices, a budget would be paramount in order to avoid mistakes and overruns. Some professional advice might be helpful.

Take Action

> **Step 1**: Select the **Top Targets Mapped to Resources Needed** matrix (Fig. 5) from the back of the book. It looks like this:

Top Targets Mapped to Resources Needed™

	Resource 1	Resource 2	Resource 3	New Resource Needed	Risk: Mitigation:
Target 1					
Target 2					
Target 3					
Target 4					
Target 5					

TOP TARGETS

> **Step 2**: Using the **Vision-to-Action Framework™**, map the current resources you identified across the top of the matrix. Notice that there is one additional column. This is for identifying NEW resources needed for achieving the targets.
>
> **Step 3**: List your top five targets vertically down the matrix.
>
> **Step 4**: For each target place an X in the box of the top three resources most needed to achieve the target. Additionally,

where those resources needed are time and money, add the minimums and maximums you contemplated previously to those respective boxes.

Step 5: Contemplate the targets. Is there a new resource needed for each specific target that has not been identified as a current resource? Identify that in the column, headed New Resource Needed, that corresponds to the target.

Step 6: Contemplate the risk/obstacles associated with the targets and the resources needed. Identify any significant risk in the Risk/Obstacles column associated with the target and specify the mitigation step needed in order to minimize the risk.

Step 7: Highlight the top three resources needed for each target. Reassess your ability and willingness to invest in the resources needed. Ensure that you are willing to do so.

Chapter 5 Summary

The completion of Chapter 5 has helped you identify the resources it will take you to achieve your targets. Most people naturally think of time and money as being the most significant of these resources. This is correct. But beyond the aspects of time and money, it should help you to realize that other people and activities can be a resource to you in achieving your targets. In addition, research is invaluable in understanding how to get something accomplished. Equally important, identifying risks and creating contingency plans will mean that you have some insurance on your side. Avoiding costly mistakes is the objective here. Identifying minimum and maximum commitments you are willing to make with your time and money is an important recognition of your risk tolerances. This step, even though it is the last, is an important checkpoint to ensure that you are committed to your target. Reworking a target now to avoid over-commitments may be the right thing to do. Or, realizing that the time is right may be the most exiting part of the plan.

As you saw in the case study, careful consideration of your resources and the choices you are making is paramount. There are consequences and implications to everything you do and in Amy's case, getting expert counsel could help mitigate the risk of her choices and ensure that she is utilizing her resources in the best way possible. That kind of professional assistance may come into play during the different parts of some of your projects.

This exercise is an important learning tool for understanding the power of resources, the thought that needs to be considered for each resource needed and the risk associated with each. Mistakes can be easy to correct if they are caught early. Thinking through the implications of relying on any resource or expecting it to be there is well worth it. Likewise, thinking of your own willingness to commit your resources in a tough economic climate is well-advised. Once you have done that you can go forward with the confidence that you are aware and prepared to marshal the resources needed to succeed.

Chapter 6

Vision to Action

Have a bias toward action—let's see something happen now. You can break that big plan into small steps and take the first step right away.

—Indira Gandhi

Get Thinking

You are almost done! The hard work is behind you. Now the last step is to make your vision of achieving your targets actionable. Start with identifying the steps of a simple plan.

Even the best targets cannot be achieved without a clear execution plan so you must do this last step on paper, not in your head. This is particularly important since even the simple act of putting the steps on paper will help you see the vision come into focus.

Some targets will require many steps to achieve the final outcome but you will not get there unless you think through the initial steps and ensure the logical sequence of events. From there you can fill in the details.

To successfully complete this part of the plan it is good to review your work to this point. Review the targets you have selected and your willingness to commit your precious resources of time and money. Keep in mind all that you have done in defining all your resources, the competencies and talents you will leverage and your willingness and ability to commit yourself to the work.

Think about the first step in building the momentum you seek. Next, think of the most important step, then the easiest step and, finally, the hardest step. As you list the actions you think will be necessary in attacking each target look at the sequence of those actions and make sure it makes sense. These actions must be in an order that will allow you to see progress as each action gets completed. Brainstorm the actions to take against your targets and jot down your thoughts.

Case Study

Ray has been working at the local coffee café for the last two years. He has a high school degree but has not been able to afford college. Ray wants to go to community college and has set a goal of saving enough to begin classes in the next semester. He sees this as a worthwhile goal as he wants to continue to educate himself in the areas he is interested in: teaching and sports.

Ray believes that the Internet will be a great resource for learning more about teaching and has looked into online college courses. He is specifically interested in teaching mathematics and would also like to pick up a part-time job coaching a Little League baseball team. He is ready to lay out his action plan for both of these targets.

Ray starts with finding online resources for continuing his mathematics education and contacts his high school baseball coach to talk more about coaching Little League. He will define two subsequent steps for each of these areas and then quickly start with the first step so he can determine whether he is on the right track.

Key Learning

Ray has a worthwhile goal of continuing his education. He has identified two good opportunities in teaching and sports and further defined his targets in teaching mathematics and coaching Little League baseball. He has identified a great resource—the Internet—to help further his learning. He should also consider using the Internet to identify educational alternatives so he can identify additional steps toward building his knowledge. Contacting his high school baseball coach is an excellent first step on his path to coaching Little League baseball. He should also identify additional sources of information and set some steps for investigating this information. Setting target dates for each of these opportunities and steps will be important in order to stay on track. As this information gets better understood he will want to create a fuller action plan that clearly lays out all the steps in his plan for each opportunity.

Take Action

Step 1: Select the **Top 5 Targets: Top 3 Next Steps matrix** (Fig. 6) from the back of the book. It looks like this:

Action Plan: Top 5 Targets/Top 3 Next Steps™

		Action Step 1	Step 1 Timeframe	Action Step 2	Step 2 Timeframe	Action Step 3	Step 3 Timeframe
TARGETS	Target 1						
	Target 2						
	Target 3						
	Target 4						
	Target 5						

STEPS/TIMEFRAME

Step 2: List the top five targets vertically down the matrix.

Step 3: For each target, identify, from the brainstormed actions, the very first step necessary to achieving the target and list that under Action Step 1.

Step 5: Repeat for Action Step 2.

Step 6: Repeat for Action Step 3.

Step 7: For each action, identify a timeframe or range of time (beginning and end date) to accomplish that step. Enter this under the Timeframe column for the appropriate step.

Chapter 6 Summary

The completion of Chapter 6 represents an important step in securing your success. Without an action plan to get you going and keep you on track you are likely not to achieve your targets. Hopefully you can see the value of understanding the order and timeframe of the work to be done. Without an action plan you are likely to get off track, not know why you have not made progress or where you are getting stuck. Especially if you are working on several targets, you will want to allocate sufficient time to each step, so clearly defining an action plan is critical. You can see the value in defining the three most important steps for each target so that you can measure success early and gain confidence in those completions.

As you saw in the case study, when you have to broaden or add additional capability to your competencies you will want to clearly define the steps to secure that knowledge and understand how much time and money that will require. Also, including steps to do some advance research in an area in which you know you will need to spend additional money should be a worthwhile, early action item. This can save you significant disappointment down the line by helping you understand the reality of the effort, time and money you may have to invest. Likewise, it can provide you with ample opportunity to plan for investments you do want to make. Clarity in the planning and timing of these steps is the desired result.

This exercise is an important step in realizing your goals and aspirations. With a well-thought-out action plan, with well-conceived, prioritized targets based on opportunities that have been evaluated and aligned to your goals and aspirations, your actions will be an investment in your future. You can go forward with confidence that you are taking the steps to secure your future in the best way you know how.

Chapter 7

Build Your Blueprint Action Plan™

I've been absolutely terrified every moment of my life—and I've never let it keep me from doing a single thing I wanted to do.

—Georgia O'Keeffe

Now you can put all of your hard work into your blueprint! You've got a real plan for achieving what you want in life!

Step 1: Select the **Blueprint Action Plan**™ matrix (Fig. 7) from the back of the book. It looks like this:

Step 2:

- Using the **Vision-to-Action Framework**™ (Fig. 1), fill in your aspirations and goals, and then your opportunities and interests.
- Using the **Targets Mapped to**

Blueprint Action Plan™					
Aspirations					
Opportunities & Interests					
5 Top Targets	Target 1	Target 2	Target 3	Target 4	Target 5
Top 3 Comp/Talent Needed 1. Leverage					
2. Add					
3. Grow					
Top 3 Resources needed 1.					
2.					
3.					
First Next Step					
Timeframe					

Aspirations and Goals (Fig. 3), fill in the five number-one top targets.

- Using the **Competencies/Talents Identified to Top 5 Targets** (Fig. 4), fill in the competencies you have identified for each target. If a competency is blank, fill in "N/A."
- Using the **Top Targets Mapped to Resources** (Fig. 5), fill in the top three resources needed for each target.
- Using the **Top 5 Targets: Top 3 Next Steps** matrix (Fig. 6), select step one for each target and fill it in. Select the timeframe for step one and fill it in.

Congratulations!
You have created your Blueprint Action Plan™!

Chapter 7 Summary

Well done! You have created your own blueprint. Think of that. What an accomplishment. It has been hard work but will yield you great benefits. You now have the power of choice in your hands. You have the certainty of knowing that your plans are well-connected.

Look at the Vision-to-Action Framework™ together with your Blueprint Action Plan™. You started with the Vision-to-Action Framework™. This is a valuable representation of where you wanted to go in terms of life aspirations and goals. You added opportunities to achieve those aspirations and goals with the knowledge of your values, competencies, talents and resources.

Taking that several steps further you crystallized your opportunities into actionable targets—specific things that you identified and evaluated. You assessed those targets against your aspirations and goals for best fit. Then, to better ensure your success, you identified your existing competencies and talents that could be leveraged and complementary competencies that will need to be broadened and deepened.

And even more, you identified competencies you needed to grow. Next you identified resources needed to achieve each target; some resources you have and others may be new. In both the competencies and resources-needed areas you further identified risks to watch out for and mitigation plans to minimize the risk. This was done to help enhance your chance of success.

Then, in order to bring your vision to action, you identified the action plan that will get you started down the road. And, FINALLY, you pulled it all together in a blueprint so that you could see your plan clearly laid out with all your choices. How many people have done that? You are now ready to begin taking action through well-thought-out direction!

Chapter 8

Get Busy!

Inaction breeds doubt and fear. Action breeds confidence and courage. If you want to conquer fear, do not sit home and think about it. Go out and get busy.

—Dale Carnegie

As you begin to execute your action plan, you will want to chart your progress and adjust your timeframes and thinking. The first three steps of your execution plan toward any of your targets will give you a good idea of progress, timing, successes and obstacles. Use the action plan to chart your progress and assess your progress regularly to make adjustments. Reset dates if necessary and track your progress. Identify additional steps as you make progress. The more steps you can identify in advance, the better your focus and understanding of all that it will take to achieve success. If progress slows, look again at your action plan and determine if you have taken the necessary steps. Assess obstacles and determine how to correct or work around them. If at some point a target is not achievable, go back through the steps and select another target. Remember that some things may just need better timing, but it shouldn't deter you from working against one or more other targets!

Appendix

Forms for
Blueprint Your Future

If you want larger versions of the charts in the Appendix for personal use, feel free to enlarge them using a scanner or copier, or by simply redrawing them on a piece of paper.

Please also visit www.blueprintyourfuture.com for automated tools.

Vision to Action Framework™

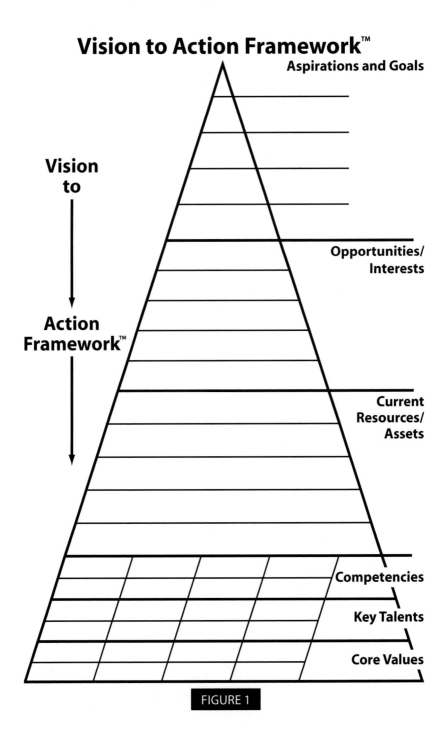

FIGURE 1

Target Indentified to Opportunities/Interest™

OPPORTUNITIES

	Opportunity 1	Opportunity 2	Opportunity 3	Opportunity 4	Opportunity 5
Target 1					
Target 2					
Target 3					

TARGETS

FIGURE 2

Targets Mapped to Aspirations/Goals™

ASPIRATIONS/GOALS

	Aspirations/Goals 1	Aspirations/Goals 2	Aspirations/Goals 3	Aspirations/Goals 4	Aspirations/Goals 5
Opportunity 1					
Opportunity 2					
Opportunity 3					
Opportunity 4					
Opportunity 5					

OPPORTUNITIES

FIGURE 3

Competencies/Talents Identified to Top 5 Targets™

	Target 1	Target 2	Target 3	Target 4	Target 5
1. Leverage existing competencies and talents	Leverage	Leverage	Leverage	Leverage	Leverage
2. Broaden/deepen an existing competency	Add	Add	Add	Add	Add
3. Grow new or different competency	Grow	Grow	Grow	Grow	Grow
Risk:					
Mitigation:					

FIGURE 4

Top Targets Mapped to Resources Needed™

TOP TARGETS	Resource 1	Resource 2	Resource 3	New Resource Needed	Risk: Mitigation:
Target 1					
Target 2					
Target 3					
Target 4					
Target 5					

FIGURE 5

Action Plan: Top 5 Targets/Top 3 Next Steps™

STEPS/TIMEFRAME

TARGETS	Action Step 1	Step 1 Timeframe	Action Step 2	Step 2 Timeframe	Action Step 3	Step 3 Timeframe
Target 1						
Target 2						
Target 3						
Target 4						
Target 5						

FIGURE 6

Blueprint Action Plan™ FIGURE 7

Aspirations					
Opportunities & Interests					
5 Top Targets	Target 1	Target 2	Target 3	Target 4	Target 5
Top 3 Comp/Talent Needed 1. Leverage					
2. Add					
3. Grow					
Top 3 Resources needed 1.					
2.					
3.					
First Next Step					
Timeframe					

For more information please visit
www.blueprintyourfuture.com